Burnt Sienna Sky

Jackie Smith

A catalogue record for this book is available from the National Library of Australia

Copyright © 2022 Jackie Smith

All rights reserved. No part of this publication may be reproduced, stored in a retrieval system, or transmitted in any form or by any means, electronic, mechanical, photocopying, recording or otherwise without prior permission of the author.

Publisher:
Inspiring Publishers
P.O. Box 159, Calwell, ACT Australia 2905
Email: publishaspg@gmail.com
http://www.inspiringpublishers.com

National Library of Australia Cataloguing-in-Publication entry

Author: Smith, Jackie

Title: **Burnt Sienna Sky**/*Jackie Smith*

ISBN: 978-1-922792-76-1 (Print)
ISBN: 978-1-922792-77-8 (eBook)

When not writing poetry, Jackie Smith is a freelance journalist, editor and proof-reader and marketing graduate based in Brisbane, QLD, Australia.

She has appeared as a featured artist at Redcliffe Writers' Open Mic, Fellowship of Australian Writers Queensland, Wynnum Library and Queensland Poetry's Volta following the release of her debut book, *The Nostalgia Collection*.

Burnt Sienna Sky is her second full-length collection of poems.

To connect with Jackie online, visit the below link:
https://linktr.ee/jackiesmithwrites

Other Books Also by This Author
The Nostalgia Collection

Mum and Dad,

Thank you.

For everything.

Table of Contents

The Fringe-Dwellers 11
Yours Truly 12
Wonder 13
Self-Portrait 16
Memory...19
Airplane Musings 21
Blind Ballerina (After Alicia Alonso) 24
Glow 26
Alive..28
Choose Your Own Adventure 29
Afraid of the Dark..31
For Laura 34
Constellations..35
Belong 36
Timeless 38
The Colour of His Love 40
Alien Encounters 42
He is … (Dad's Poem) 43
Forgive Me 45
Helios 46
Lightning in the Sand 48
All-Nighter 50
Darling Girl (For Sidnee)...51

Blood Moon 53
Silence 55
Intention/Reflection 56
Optimism 57
Now 59
Break the Mould 61
Apocalypse (After Robert Frost) 63
Faith 65
Falsehoods 68
Vows 70
Thank You 72
The Fall of Icarus (After Bruegel) 75
Shapeshifter 77
Blank Page (After Ross Gay & Gwendolyn Brooks'
Sorrow Is Not My Name) 79
The Unicorn & The Phantom 81
Never Again 83
Little Miracles 85
Pretty 87
Tranquility 89
Sea Monster 91
Quiet 93
I Remember (A Victim's Lament) 95
Legend 96
Hurricane 97
Mystic 99

Black Dahlia 101
Ashes.. 102
New World.. 104
The End 106
If You're Listening (For Nan) 107
Sunrise 110
Sunlight.. 111
Heirloom.. 112
Grave of Yesterdays... 114
Warrior... 115
Warrior Pt 2 118
Free Falling 120
White on White... 123
Code Breaker... 126
Black Flamingo... 127
I Wish I Were A Feather 129
Daffodils... 130
Echoes in the Vibration 131
Wait for Me 132
Martyr (Joan of Arc) 133
I Am.. 136
Glitter... 138
Forever... 139
Call Me... 140
On Existence 141
Mute.. 142

Songbird 143
Wildfire 144
The Enigma 145
This Place 146
Mathematics of Courage 148
Selway Avenue 150
Lost in a Lullaby (After Lewis Carroll's Alice in Wonderland) 152
Nightmare 154
Speed of Sound 155
Too Late 156
Broken Wing 157
Storybook Affair 158
Paradox 159
Worthy 160
Flickering Flame 162
Impossible 164
Madness 165
Mother Nature 166
Bouquet 167
Pedestal (After Neil Hilborn) 168
Spirit 170
Symphony 172
Perfect Imperfections 174
Aurora 176
Notes 179

The Fringe-Dwellers

We are the fringe-dwellers,
wandering free,
the wallflowers, immigrants and outcasts.

We sit on the edge of eternity,
watching the stars welcome the sun in its dazzling blue.

We meet at midnight,
far from prying eyes that begrudge our nomadic existence,
hold each other tight in the loving embrace of makeshift family.

We shield ourselves against the icy hand of the first snowfall,
fires' embers having long met their ashy death
in a war we never wanted to fight,
never wanted to win,
never wanted to lose.

And as the dawn melts into the horizon,
we surrender,
rejoice in the birth of a radiance unexplainable
to those who reject the promise of tomorrow, and refuse to accept
a future we will never understand.

Yours Truly

I read the letter
you wrote,
Took comfort in your crumpled paper,
touched my lips to the tear-stained ink you left behind like an imprint on my heart,
and pictured the last time I held your hand.
I traced your spider-like font that only I could read,
handwriting half-formed in cursive,
the way I finished your sentences,

assured yet uncertain.

Imagined your hand holding the pen
as you pondered over the final sentence,
trying to mould your words into meaning that wouldn't
shatter my heart even while it was breaking.

Because if this is the end of the story as we know it
Where was my beginning,
The middle where I got to love you more fiercely than
I ever knew was possible
Even as we reach this impossible finale,
and sign the page
yours truly.

Wonder

I am the glass slipper
abandoned on the ballroom stair
pouring rain glistening
on the heel.

The rose with the last petal falling
Before the curse
is broken.

I am the clock
that strikes
at midnight
turning the page
in the fairy tale.

I am the northern star
lighting the way
to Neverland
the knife at the villain's throat
at the end of the movie.

I am the catalyst
and the exception
the dream of everything
you once thought of as right.
The journey
and the inspiration
the soldiers marching
at night
across battle planes unexplored.

I am the desert
Without water
the genie in the lamp
granting all your wishes
in the hope that they may one day
come true.

I am the imagination
and the symphony
the memory
of a childhood
not so lost
in the forest
following crumbs to
find my way home.

I am the imagination

the promise of all
that can
and will happen
if you only
let go.

And take a moment
to believe
in the impossible.

Self-Portrait

In the early morning,
My muscles take their own sweet time to unfurl
from the cocoon of sleep
before they're ready to re-join the land of the living.

I stretch and pulse
Creak and moan
Nerve ending always on edge,
Ready for the next fall from
Grace,
From introspection
From the sidewalk as I run too fast and trip
On an invisible crack,
Trying to keep pace with time
That never stops moving.

Experts once told me that every step I take
It's worth ten of yours.

So I've spent the last few decades playing catch up
In a race you didn't even know you were running.

You see, this life is a marathon,
All barricades and hurdles,
Goalposts placed so far across a field
I'll never quite reach the finish line.

Never quite be what you class as normal.

But why would you want to be normal
If it means living up to someone else's expectations
If it means watching the stars
instead of dancing on the moon
across galaxies and timelines you never thought
possible?

This world was never really meant for someone like me
Pushing the boundaries to find what lies beyond the safe
    and comfortable.

So I've created a world of my own,
Built from the castles made of sand you left behind
A piece of heaven
In this hellish descent into the unknown
The home of unrealised dreams and potential just waiting for
You to return and take the opportunity you forgot you once had.

Because the globe is only round until you start to mould it with your own hands,
Take what's yours and craft it into the shape and colour of your own skin
Delicate centres and a fragile composition
Ready to jump and fall,
To fly and fail
To relish in the night if it means you have
A chance to touch the sun
If only once
If only fleetingly
In this life that was never meant to last forever.

Memory

This place screams
"I'm haunted"
like it's a term of endearment
bestowed by a loved one.

Once crowded chambers echo the
laughter of ghosts
long abandoned
follow the spirits lightly
on tiptoe as though
we're running away from the dark.

I
I scream,
"I'm haunted"
like it's a term of endearment,
full of grace and beauty
and all that is right with the world

I trace the walls like arteries of your sacred heart
And linger in promises unbroken,
Metaphors unwritten

I still compare thee to a summer's day when
All the trees have turned to grey,
Like this memory is not simply fragments
Of an overactive imagination.

Airplane Musings

I watch the sky change from grey
To pink to purple and crimson haloed in gold
From this cold, cramped airplane
On my way to meet you,
The idealised version of who I want to
Spend the rest of my life with and
I can't help thinking of the word love,
How in all its different interpretations and dictionary meanings it's
The term we use for a feeling we cannot name.

Desperate to belong we cast our expectations on a single star,
And hope that someone in our far-flung universe will keep it safe and
    warm,
Let it heal the scars of their own broken heart
Spark the embers of a new beginning before they become lost
In the fog of a forgotten ending.

Up here,
Thousands of kilometres above the Earth as it rotates
On its never-ending axis,
We become caught in the potential
Of the impossible
Believing that we can fly while
We're still falling

Sketch our promises in ink on stone
And hope that the storm
We're soaring into won't
Wash away their good intentions.

Cast pebbles across the lake
And throw lockets into the ocean below
to
Prove our love is limitless
To prove we're fighting for something
Worth drowning for.

I write these words
Over the graves
Of every hopeless romantic
Who has come before
As I trek ever-closer to you
And I don't want them to get lost in
Translation when I think of the word love.

Because when we speak we create our own language
Where there's no room for error I adhere
To every stolen cliché
When I tell you
If I look into
Your eyes
I see a mirror reflecting my soul.

That I've spent years picking up the fragments of my heart's
Shattered puzzle only for you to help me see the magic in
What's broken and beautiful.

That the static inside my brain clears in
Perfect reception when I hear your voice down
The coiled phone lines.

Even though we're miles
Apart,
Living in distant galaxies
And right now you're nothing more
Than a figment of my imagination
Come true
I hope I get to make that journey.
Some day.
Some day soon.

Blind Ballerina

(After Alicia Alonso)

I etch each line of you
I cannot see
trace each feature of your silhouette
in the movements of my dance
so I will not forget
the echoes of your love.

How my home is within your heart as
I twirl and leap and jump into another's arms
The beat of your music
residing in the mincing steps I take
across the stage
knowing that if
the curtain were to fall
upon these shadowed eyes
and I could no longer hear
the applause of strangers
watching my graceful ways,

You would be there to help me rise
And we would
        Dance
                Dance
                        Dance
in this soft circle of love
and wistful hearts
until the day the world stops spinning
and the light's shadow
fades to dust.

Glow

I look up at the night sky
watch as inky black fades into pale charcoal
once the last of the fireworks has farewelled the year we've left behind
and think of all that is possible in this
yet untarnished future.

In these moments so fresh and new,
I'm untouched by the catalyst
of mistakes long overdue.

I want to set fire
to the regrets of yesterday
see broken promises
smoulder in the embers like a letter
to a long-forgotten lover.

I want to rid this body of all
Its pain and suffering,
Let the edges turn blue with the heat of a fire
Left untended.

I want to strike a match to these
Unfulfilled plans,
Lose myself in the warmth of the flame.

I want to set alight these stories untold
Reveal their secrets in the exploding comets above.

I want to scorch your skin with my mark
as proof of my existence,
relish in the smoke that builds from this candle
as we say goodbye to those who never got the chance to
get old
or watch the sun rise over the mountain
and set this world ablaze with the
lingering light
of Hope.

So when the brightness wavers
I want to become the flame
Rather than the ash discarded
On the wind.

For I am the Phoenix
And together we will rise
Again
Again
And again,
… until the end
Of Time.

Alive

A serpent's kiss
Of impending doom
Sparks the end of
the world as we know it.

The planet's ablaze but there's
peace in the silence
a cacophony of white noise echoing the
drums from nearby explosions.

I walk this decaying street,
alone and unafraid,
soot-stained and bloody,
but barely,
just barely alive.

The world is turning
at a rapid pace and I feel dizzy trying to keep up.

But here on the edge of hell,
where ice crystalises alongside lava,
I am alive.

Choose Your Own Adventure

We exist in a universe with no centre,
Stars flickering off balance in an endless night.

We speak in words unspoken,
languages made up in a time and space of ancient traditions
and rituals we can never even begin to understand,
follow the torchlight in the dark, seeking answers to unasked questions.

We walk the same path
Trodden by ancestors long passed before our time,
Wearing shoes always a size too big,
each time expecting to reach a different destination,
no compass,
no navigation.

We keep secrets close to our chests,
Behind locked doors, in cages with rusty locks and broken keys,
guarded by the bruises that left invisible marks on skin.

Like birds we lose our song,
no choir to sing along.

Shattered on the floor, we judge our actions

by watching others raise a bar
rather than climb the ladder of our own success.
Like déjà vu, we follow the same actions,
Make the same plans over and over.
Don't they call that insanity?

And still we persevere,
fight an endless war to which we
can't change the outcome.

They say this life is short,
But I don't believe it's true.
The candle's flame may flicker, but its embers will remain.

And if one day years from now,
I come to you in dreams,
Remember this story, as I told it true.
The next chapter belongs to you.

For if the universe has no centre,
how can our history of time,
ever be brief?

Afraid of the Dark

I am not afraid of the dark,
the rich indigo beauty of
the night sky as it eclipses the sun
every evening.

I watch the comets speed across a navy canvas,
Splitting the space time continuum
Filling it with light so bright
I question if I should believe in a god
I can't confirm exists.

In the shadows
Where the grim reaper lurks
Baying for blood
As fairies dance at his feet,
Shielding secrets from prying eyes.

The wolves howling at the crescent moon,
Haunting my dreams

The noir swan as it arches its back
across crystal blue waters,
the panther as she hunts her kill with onyx eyes.

I'm not afraid of the deep unknown,
Abandoned islands, the midnight waves as they
Search the shore for a safe resting place.

The raven as it whispers against velvet wind,
The violet backed starling languishing in imperial purple.

The black flamingo who refuses to
Shine in watercolour,
Relishing in its violent hues.

The exact shade of melancholy
When all the colour leeches from the world.

The ink that flows from this rusty pen,
Conjuring words on paper when my mind is racing
And I cannot sleep.

No, I'm not afraid of the dark,
Imperfect though it may be.

Because in the dark,
There is you,
The volcanic lightning on the mountain top,
Embers among the smoke in the ashes before it clears,
The lifeforce within reminding me,

With soothing words and gentle caresses,
That sometimes it's okay
To admit I am
Afraid of the dark.

For Laura

In the darkness
you were the light
that led the way through an endless tunnel.

In the storm
You were the refuge
the safe place I could shelter
waiting for the thunder to pass overhead.

When I couldn't see the summer sun
You were there to show me the constellations
Align.

You were the one who told me
That everything would be alright
Even when you didn't know if that was true.

You were the voice on the end of the phone line
When I was lost and searching for home.

You were a sister to this only child,
You taught me the value of family
And for that I will be forever grateful.

Constellations

The stars were asleep last night,
So I couldn't write by the light of the haloed moon
let it fill my pen with the ink
of her iridescent glow as she allowed her brilliant sister
to slumber.

I never considered myself a night owl,
Burning the candle down to the wick
Until I looked to the stars for inspiration
Found purpose in their flaming mystique
Turned crystal by the hollowed gulf of our existence.

The sun rose early this morning,
To reveal the ghost of Luna lingering in pale shades of coral
Dancing flamingo on a distant ocean I cannot see from my west facing
    window
As the heat of the day warms my back like a blazing fire
Thaws bones in the winter.

I couldn't write by the weary stars last night,
So today I'll write by the dawn
Let its kaleidoscopic aura fill my page with a prism of possibility,
Follow its amber iris
In search of treasure and weave these silver-spun into
A glimmer
Of gold.

Belong

On a starlit morning,
When the sky was the colour of new snow
Fresh, white, clean, and filled with promise
As dew drops fell with the rising sun,

I wake
From
Foggy visions and fragile slumber
To anguished screams and curses louder than the silence
I've left behind.

I walk
this world on shattered glass
Bloody feet on stepping-stone.

I unravel
the night within the day
pull at strings
And hope that the moon will reveal a place for me
Among your Heaven.

Because in the dark,
When dreams become promises made to the
Gods above,
I count my wishes
On every single star I see because
All I want is to have them tell me
I belong.

Timeless

I write this anthem to a sky full of stars
ask it what it wants to be as though I don't already know
the answer is
"Infinite".

Like the galaxy waits until the dawn
to echo the halo
of the everlasting moon.

Like the angels' chorus doesn't reverberate
in the birds' song
as it bids farewell
to the day,
heralds in the twilight blue
honouring rainbows unfiltered
from starry lakes.

As though I don't already know
Infinity is not a place we will ever reach
but a number we can't count to
a feeling we can't capture
no matter how hard we try
because it's greater than everything.

Every single thing
That has ever come before this moment
that touches the soul with its loving gentle caress
and ignites the fires
in a heart that only
wants to understand something
other than stone.
I write this anthem
in violet crescendo,
ask myself
what I want to be
like I don't already know
the answer is
"Infinite."

The Colour of His Love

"Do you speak in sleep my dear
Or do you dream of Love?"

I wake
To a world bright with scarlet rage,
Listen from shadows deeper than
the grave as she shields herself
From his temper frayed,
Lamenting time lost to youth and a life
Misspent by her side.

He stains her skin the way you paint the glass of
   a Church window
Her cheek electric with the colour of his love
As she lays her shattered dreams made of diamonds at his feet,
prays for release from this living nightmare.

I would save her if I could
Release her from the chains that bind her to the demon
She once called her God.

So I direct my telescope to the Heavens in hope of raising Hell
Shout to the reckless angels to wield their trumpets in defence of
All the lost souls who can't find their way home.

When war is won,
We'll embrace these cosy winters,
Fire laced with sunsets
And I will whisper
"Do you speak in sleep my dear,
Or do you dream
Of Love?"

Alien Encounters

In my darkest dreams
when the sky is still
a smoky haze
the creature of unknown affinity appears.

He takes my hand
Guides me out into the charcoal smudge of day
and asks me to follow him,
Together we ride the indigo night
Drink our fill of shimmering, showering secrets.

We journey to the moon and call it Saturn
look down on the restlessness of humanity
with pity and grace.

We carve the treetops into the horizon
As the city wakes
Languish in the violet of the rainbow
As it dances across the ocean.

As the sun rises,
We melt into its honeyed dews of
Silver and gold
Before sleep overtakes us and
I'm lost
In the beauty of this world.

He is ... (Dad's Poem)

He asks me to write a poem
For him as though he isn't already in
Every word I write.

As though he isn't the ink that
Fills my pen with blue-black scratchings
At midnight
When the wolves howl at my door
And the owl shrieks of danger
And torment in the middle of a storm.

He wants me to speak of my love
For him but I struggle to find the words
With only 26 letters and a million variations.

He is the echo to my call
Across the mountain top
The sounding board to my innermost thoughts,
A safe space when
I can't find my way through the dark.

The match that lights my flame within,
The strength I turn to when I fall,
The encouragement I need to rise again.

He is the home
I return to time and time
And time Again.

Forgive Me

What is forgiveness
but a promise to do better,
an apology to the universe or
proof
you once had the intention to make a difference.

Like you never intended to burn my soul with
Your fiery gaze,
Never tore my innocent heart on those
Reckless Days
In June.

Like you never intended to exchange my love
for your contempt
as I fell deep for your ill-written words

Like I never allowed myself to believe I wasn't worthy of you
Never made myself your sun
Instead of the star in this new beginning.

Forgive me,
It was my mistake

I'll do better
This time around.

Jackie Smith

Helios

I didn't think there'd be a time
when I missed the sun
its glorious rays sinking
into my skin,
the way your smile
lights up the new morning,
before the birds wake from dreams.

We walk these fields
and valleys
in search of the northern star
no longer dance in the light
of a new moon
that promised freedom
on the edge of tomorrow
when we took heaven
… and made it better.

When we weren't losing our grip
on the world
as it spins on its axis.

When I say I miss the sun
I mean the feeling that courses
through my veins every time
you look my way,
leaving electricity
in your wake.

I hope that one day you will return
to the comfort of my arms
and turn every delicate fear
that creeps into my dreams at night
into nothing more than
a memory.

I hope we face these new challenges
with armour stronger than steel
ignite the passion of an army rejoicing
in the power of our strength.

But most of all
when it's over,
I hope we dance
among the stars in a distant universe
and can call heaven our own
once again.

Lightning in the Sand

Butterflies dance upon windowsills,
in rainstorms,
lightning in the sand.

Delighting in these fractured moments,
Of broken promises
stolen from all of your yesterdays.

If what glitters is not gold,
how can I touch you
with these tarnished hands?

Black sapphire
Coal-dipped fingerprints
I bruise you with a single touch
Can't kiss you like there is no tomorrow,
Because we don't know what the future holds.

You are the raven-hearted vine
Creeping
Over the foundations of this haunted house,
Chase the spirit
Of our love
In the last days,

Before it died.
Blood drips like acid from the
Edges of my shattered history
And still I love you
Even though every
Part of me lingers, splintered by your Ghost.

All-Nighter

The first time I stayed up all night
We'd been to a concert
Entered in the dark of an old run-down building
That probably used to be a factory
but is now home to
Underground dancers who find their self-worth
In the tell-tale reflection of lipstick-stained mirrors
And the heavy thump of a song they never bothered
   to learn the words to.

When the fragile smoke of a too-crowded room turned bright with
   florescence,
We made our way back into a world beating with colour
Lost in a city I could never really call my own,
I discovered what it is
To be
Breathing.

Darling Girl

(For Sidnee)

Darling girl,
I see you
curled on the floor
of your room
shrouded in the darkness of your
broken thoughts.

Darling girl
What do you see when you look
Into the mosaic scars of my eyes?

Darling girl
I know you're lost
Drowning in the ocean of adolescence
Struggling to preserve a life worth living.

Darling girl,
I wish I could show you
What I see when you

Look at me
How your light shines brighter
than any of the stars in this
Endless galaxy.

Darling girl,
Your heart is bigger than the sun
Deeper than the depths of the hell
You're in right now.
Darling girl,
You're not all lost at sea
You are the sea,
You are more than the sea
And you have the power
To be more than you ever thought you could be.

Darling girl,
I see you.
Do you see me?

Blood Moon

Blood moon,
I watch you
High and mighty with your rosy hue,
Desolate until the dawn.

Summer solstice on a winter's eve,
Brilliant and true,

You stain the darkness with your ruby glow,
Herald of evil,
tempest of doom.

Blood moon,
I bathe in your mirrored reflection,
Let it cleanse me to the core,
Wash away unspoken sins.

Dance with the devil
like I'm an immortal
looking curiously from above,

Watch the stars drink
their fill,
soak up the echoes of your crimson glory.

Blood moon,
Reveal your murderous intentions,
bruised fingertips upon your skin.

You invite evil to your door,
sing as the witches' brew simmers
and wolves pose questions to their new God.

Blood moon,
what do you say in reply
when they lament the chaos of humans?

Do you soothe their weary tears
with whispers on the wind,
comfort them by the light of your fire?

Blood moon,
There is none holier than you
I pray in the shadows of your light.

And when you rise,
Delicate and bright,
I hope the sun trembles in your wake.

Silence

In the end
there will be silence,
the gentle whisperings of passion,
the hum of a newborn day disappearing as
it no longer wakes
in the summer sun.

In the end,
there will be love,
fresh like a daisy
bright as the crystal sky
dizzy like a spinning top
we just can't slow down.

In the end,
The globe won't deafen us
in a loud cacophony of noise and violence.
The army will raise its white flag in defiance,
As we lay down to sleep.

In the end,
there will be silence.

Intention/Reflection

If 4000 years from now,
You read these scribbled missives with wry tongues
And acid laced gazes
I want you to know that we never meant
to let you inherit an earth
already ablaze with uncontrollable flames.

We never meant to extinguish the light from the land
you now call home
reached for the gold and let it tarnish
Never would have witnessed the sun and
try to harness its power with our forceful hands.

We wouldn't have watched the sky
Become bruised
with the reflection of
our Fragile pain
Etching anger into the corners of our cosmos.

We never would have explored the forest,
delved deep into its evergreen heart
only to later see it burn crimson.

We never would have destroyed
What you worked so hard to create.

(I hope)

Optimism

My nan once told me there's no such thing as the word can't.
And I believed her.

This human race runs too fast, always trying to catch up to
time that's already ticking away, spinning endlessly
as storm clouds gather on the edge of a world designed to throw us off kilter,
we lament the grey,
forgetting that lightning creates shimmering sculptures in sand
unmarred by the rough hands of a society that doesn't know when to stop.

Slow down and revel in the early morning light,
and after every flood there is a rainbow and I want
to live in the infinite colour of its never ending palette
of indigo blue, emerald green and the blazing shimmering red
of the sunset on the horizon.

Have you ever seen such wonderous shades?

I want to walk in the footsteps of those who told me no,
Fly above hilltops and trees to reach goals they said I would never reach,
Dreams they said should never see the light of day
In a brand-new morning

Where everything has changed
And nothing stays the same,
Unless you let it.

Take comfort in the darkness only the weeping moon
Knows better than you know yourself.

I want to stand where others have fallen.
From bullets shattering in the hearts of innocents who never asked
To be part of this war raging within you.

After the camera flashes,
I want to be the one standing beside you in glorious cinematic technicolour.

My nan once told me there's no such word as can't
And I believed her,
So while you may see the dark of the evening,
I lose myself in the stars,
In the knowledge
That I am enough.

I want to be more than enough.

Now

This is the moment
Right now
is the time
when we must decide
whether we should
fight or fly.

As though soaring above
Making friends with the clouds
Isn't a way of choosing
To rise above.

To stand
where others have fallen

To walk
to the top of the mountain
and scream into the void
as though silence doesn't exist.

To build
upon the walls
others have constructed around them
break down the barriers of
shattered hearts and dreams.

To recognise
That the opinion of my enemy
Doesn't have to be my own.

To witness
all the colours of the rainbow
And live in the light of their endless slumber.

To rid
the sky of all its grey
so the sun has a place to shine.

This is the moment
We begin.

Break the Mould

They say bloom where you are planted
But I've been waiting here for hours,
Counting off the days
As they become months
That slowly change into years.

The seasons change,
But I do not grow
Flowers wilt,
Sorrow turns
To joy
To excitement
To harmony
To love.

With the echo of each tender moment
and the world moves forward
leaving all our yesterdays behind because they don't
make us what we're yet to become.

Take shelter from the storm
Languish and laugh as we dance in the rain
And the knowledge that every single second of this life
Is our time to make it our own
And the clocks run forwards not back

So I cannot,
Must not
remain here,
In this abandoned garden
Surrounded by the weeds
But rise
With the sun
Like there is no limit
To the sky
Because there isn't
And time … time forever moves on.

I have the power to move
To grow
To seek
To change
With it.

Apocalypse

(After Robert Frost)

I don't know yet how the world will end
In dark grey and silhouettes.
But before it does,
I want to paint its curves in all the shades of colour.

Pink, like a newborn baby minutes after they enter the world,
Yellow like your honeyed eyes as we took in the sun after an eclipse.
Green like the envy in a werewolf's eyes as he contemplates immortality
Blue, like the grief I will feel in leaving you.

I want to dance in the wake of promises fulfilled,
    ride the comet's tail across the heavens.

I want to dine with the gods,
Drink champagne as they set the earth on fire amid chaos and fury.
I want to listen to the angels sing,
Immerse myself in the sounds of their melodic chorus.

I want to love like tomorrow will never come,
Because it won't, lay down beside you and whisper all the sweet
    nothings in your ear so you know
You are everything to me. And more.

When the darkness comes to take me, I will welcome his icy touch
Close my eyes to sleep in the devil's slumber as I watch the stars shine
Like crystals on a shadowy moon
And I will know that I have done all I can,
In this land of ice and flame
My life mattered.
I mattered.
I matter
We all matter.

Faith

I don't believe in the presence of
an Almighty God,
holding court
over Paradise
gated with pearls and a
symphony of angels.

I don't believe in life after death
Where you can return to a world
that I am not a part of any longer,
because I must believe
that if you had the chance to return
you never would have left.

Never left these deserted halls
Of a house
That is no longer yours
But
Will always be yours.

Because it's the house of my childhood,
Of Christmas and New Year.

I don't believe that you would choose
to miss
the beginning
of a new generation
who will grow up knowing your name
but not the sound of voice
rallying 7 children
with your soft tones and gentle gaze
as Summer brought us to your door.

I don't believe
In the power of an Almighty God
But I refuse to believe you are
Now nothing but ash
From a burning fire.

You are the light in the
New moon,
The stardust as it fills
The night sky
The rainbow
That eclipses
The sun after a storm.

You are the shadow behind me,
The driving force behind the rain
The echo of
The thunder

Telling me
I cannot give up.
And I won't,
Because you are here
In the fragment of memory
The high of childish joy
The ink
That flows from this pen.
I will not give up.

Falsehoods

It was a bright Autumn Day
The air cool to the bone
when I recognised the tarnished gold of your friendship,
once slick with silver and clearer than a diamond
lost to the storm.

You handed me the poisoned chalice and
I drank from it greedily
Savoured your wine
not realising it was killing me
From within.

But we were young back then,
You the queen of this kingdom we built
For ourselves
And I a slave to your every whim.
A fool for your missives and tall tales told with
Fervour,
Not understanding your story was not
My own to narrate.

I hung on every word you spoke
Sought validation in your serpent smile,
Took each bile-laced letter and held it tight.
Naive and trusting to a fault.

Your speech was reckless
Cut deeper than the knife you held
With one hand behind your back
As you watched my innocence fade to nothing
Crumble to the ground and dissolve with the fragile
Light of the new morning dew.

And though it's been years,
I still think of that day,
When your well-intended phrases stung like the bee
Searching for a flower.
Now I write my own story
Penned from the shadows of your fire,
Until your lie is nothing but fiction
A fleeting memory,
a speck of dust
As truth will overcome.

Vows

In the beginning,
There was love,
The warm endurance
Of the planets aligning.

As the galaxy changed and moved
With the sun,
An eclipse of violent nights
Across the desert.

And so,
Today and forever more,
I vow to be your northern star
When you're all at sea
In the cold darkness
Of the abyss.

I will be the feathered wings on which
You rise
Every time you fall.

The hand upon your shoulder
As you cry
Crystal tears,

Frozen in a time,
And space you cannot see
Beyond.

I will be the shelter
That you call home.
Home
From now and forever more
This is the beginning.

Thank You

There are not enough words in the English language
to describe all you've taught me,
so I write this as an acknowledgement of all I remember.

1.
How you took my hand and showed me
The way when I couldn't find the stars in the dark.

2.
To understand the promise in the unknown
if I only have the courage to try.

3.
That roadblocks aren't a sign to stop,
But a detour as we find another path Aound.

4.
The beauty of taking life slow,
watching the sun set across twilight skylines.

5.
How to speak when others are silent and embrace the quiet of dreams.

6.
How you watched with graceful pride as I took first steps
in making all my wishes come true

7.
How to laugh
In moments of newfound joy
Rather than cry for all that is lost

8.
When to listen to those much wiser than me,
Seek truth among the lies.

9.
That there is no fear in failing
if you took the chance to fly.

10.
And to never compromise myself
To muster the strength within to go on when
Others say the game is lost,
Embrace the glory of tomorrow as
An opportunity to start again

For all these lessons and a million more
I thank you.
And hope that some day
I can be just like you,
Teach my unborn children what can happen if
You trust
That all is possible.

The Fall of Icarus

(After Bruegel)

We walk the streets of fallen angels
debris masking the footsteps of gods
who have come before.

Ill-fitting shoes hide the blisters
Forming from soft feet
on rough cobblestones
as ships sail the green jade ocean wave
in search of treasures in undiscovered land,
far off grey horizon.

A promise
of all that can
and will
Exist
In dark worlds
Where light is sparse
And envy shades the water
in tones of bottle green,
blue and winter white.

As swimmers bathe upon the shoreline
Languishing at water's edge
Gazing up at coal-smudged clouds in wonder,
Questioning why Icarus chose
To fly
Towards the sun,
When he could have
Stayed,
wax-dipped
wings abandoned
on the mossy sea floor,
among the stars
that light the heavens
and watch the sun from afar,
shine on a new day
dawning violet blue.

Shapeshifter

The world is full of triangles,
And I am the circle that does not fit.
I am comprised of a never-ending spiral,
all soft curves and frames made safe from years of practice
building up a defence against the sharp corners of your acid tongue and cutting blades
meant to wound my most delicate bruises.

I am the vortex you get tangled in
the shapeshifter trying to mould myself to your innermost desires.
I am the hurricane, the twister hellbent on renewal.
The lightning in the storm
when the stars have fled from the night,
creating dreamscapes in someone else's sky.

I am the ocean and the wave,
Teasing the shore
The rainbow after the rain,
A prism so full of colour you can't help but see the light
Guiding you to a pot of gold.

I am the ghost of tomorrow,
The soothing kiss of your mother's lips chasing away
The spirit of your nightmares.

The softening of the edges in this brave new centre
We take on each new morning
When we wake
To discover
The miracle
Of tulips
Growing in the snow.

Blank Page

*(After Ross Gay & Gwendolyn Brooks'
Sorrow Is Not My Name)*

Sorrow is not my name
calling back to winter as we take these final
steps into heady days of new spring.

My heart is but a fractured compass
lighting way to an endless dawn.

These invisible scars are not the
shape of my soul
that lies beneath
simply a reminder
of what once was
and what the future may hold
if I wrap this discarded
skeleton around my
frozen silhouette
like armour built for my defence.

Take this solitary second
of a moment forgotten
in time,

hold it in my hand like thunder
after the storm
allow the lightning to
fill me up
with its aura.

The promise of all that remains
If I choose to believe
That I am more
than the shadows of the fragments
that line these pages of my history,
and I can harness
the power of my story
yet to be told
through the courage of my strength
that lies within.

The Unicorn & The Phantom

I speak in whispers of gold and ivory
Tendrils curling around the air
Slowly
Delicately
Deliberately
like the smoky haze as it rises
from a well-fuelled fire,
heavy
heady
confusing yet
full of promise.

You respond in shades
of deep blue darker
than the ocean at night,
when the moon reflects
on the surface of the wave
so seamlessly
you can't quite tell the difference between up and down.

Swings and roundabouts
There's no beginning or end
to this story
glitter in the chaos of the present.

We meet on the edge of blurred photos
And memories
at sunset and sunrise
when the world seems devoid of colour we fill in the edges
like a child's drawing
no rules,
no compass
only light in the new morning
reminding us that the sun is but
a thousand stars on the horizon.

Never Again

War came in flashes
textbook snapshots and propaganda posters
outlined in burnt sienna.
As a child
I thought we had outgrown crimson poppy lined fields
Heavy with the thick, black blood of our ancestors
To become united by learning from our mistakes,
Determined not to follow in the footsteps of leaders
Who
became love-drunk on power
because they promised this would never happen again.

Now the battlefield has changed,
Green grass turned copper with age
All our forgotten black and white pictures have morphed into
A raging technicolour of TV screens
Showcasing footage of deep bunkers heaving with life
Long after the ghosts have abandoned them
Soothing strangled cries,
Cleaving to the vow
That this would never happen again.

We wake in the morning,
To dreams much more vivid than the imagination
Watch you sift through the shards of grey and ash
you once called home,
Cursing those who said
This will never happen again.
Oceans away from violent trauma
As history repeats itself
I pray in the only way I know how
Repeat the oath they vowed when
They told us never again
Never again
Never again.
But we keep finding ourselves here
Again
And again
And again.

Little Miracles

It is hard not to believe in miracles,
When you're considered one yourself,
newborn babe come to early,
singing songs that don't exist.

A speck of light in the darkness,
a fleeting flame in smoke.

The way the sky is full of colours
on summer days when light is new.

When the spring breeze is warm with heat,
rain in a thunderstorm.

A meteorite shooting through the universe,
Destined for the Earth.

The sprinkle of stars on a night sky petunia,
Golden fingerprints in the dark.
A child's laugh in the melancholy
When you're spiralling
Down
down
down

The way a heart can beat too fast
at a single look of love.

I don't know where miracles come from,
But their existence can't be denied,
they fill me from within,
keep the shadows from my door
when the world loses its glitter,
my hands shake,
and my heart removes its armour.

Pretty

I remember when I was young
standing in front of your mirror
watching you primp and preen,
play with your hair
fix an imaginary strand
fallen out of place.

How you'd walk before your closet
discarding each beautiful non-contender as you contemplated
the event you were to attend,
perfect garments lined up on the bed like forgotten loves.

You asked me what dress you should wear,
As though my opinion matters,
if this new one
- all black and delicate lace –
Makes you look pretty.

And as you stood before your reflection
Make up just right,
Lipstick a tender shade of red,
I should have told you
You're always pretty

To me,
How your smile
- rare though it may be –
Lights up the darkest night.
How your happiness matters more
To me than anything else in the world.

But I didn't,
Simply smiled at the woman
I want to become and said,
"It's nice".

Now I stand before
This mirror
In my best dress twirling around
The room like a
Hollywood star.

You watch from the doorway.
I stop, dizzy and lost in unspoken insecurities.
I ask you if I look pretty.
You say,
"You are always pretty
To me."

And my smile lights up the night.

Tranquility

I am an old soul in a new body,
Seek refuge in the familiarity of
the known rather than the darkness
that lurks beyond every corner I have yet to stumble beyond.

I err on the side of caution,
zip my delicate skin over a bruised skeleton,
surround myself in the bright
colours of other people's light
hoping that one day it will
become my own.

In this city of fallen angels,
and clipped wings,
new moons on the horizon
are just something pretty to look at,
rather than a destination.

I want to take the leap of faith everyone else is afraid of,
face the fear and do it anyway,
fall from the highest mountaintop
and surrender to the crushing weight of eternity
as it carries me to my next journey.

Everlasting sleep calls my name
But before I answer
I want to tread in the glow of the sun,
Break the chains that shackle humanity under lock and key
as the army screams bloody murder.

I want to the watch the stars as they fall
on a winter's night,
icicles dripping down their heavenly bodies.
I want joy and happiness,
Tragedy and rage.

But most of all,
When the storms are thrashing outside
And lightning chases the thunder,
When it's too loud for me to think,
Too quiet for me to breathe,
I want peace.

Sea Monster

You live in the echoes
of the deep beyond,
in myth, legend and fairy tales.

You haunt the depths of the sea,
in isolation, exclusion.
This thing,
This terrible monster from a watery grave
Only the bravest sailors hunt at midnight,
Scare children with stories of your prowess.

But if they could follow the northern star
As it shines above sunken shipwrecks,
find connection in the unknown,
embracing what they do not understand,
they too would find beauty in your power.

They would linger in the grace of your presence,
Mesmerised by the light as it shimmers on your soft skin,
Like diamonds from coal.

They wouldn't wrestle from your touch,
But revel in its warmth,
like a fire after the rain.

Jackie Smith

They'd trace every vowel in your
Strange new language,
Eager to learn your ways.

Like the cracking of an iceberg
When it feels the first taste of Spring,
They would marvel in your consonants,
Your delicate exterior hiding a heart
Fuller than the new moon.

If they could look beyond,
As I do,
They would find peace in every line
of your man-made scars.

Quiet

If I could describe the silence
that exists
in every newfound moment when you first appear,
it would be the echo
of the vibrating sun
when it creeps through the window
staining these four walls
pink
with its radiance.

These moments
when there is nothing to say
but exist in a parallel universe
where your voice can say more
than you ever
thought possible
without a single word.

The seconds before we take a single breath,
After coming up for air in this infinite
Drop of the ocean.

How I didn't see you drowning
But marvelled at the way the lightning
hits the waves
in the storm.

Like looking for the summer
in the middle of a winter frost.

How a dream can only last a minute
But stay with you
longer than a lifetime.

And I would live through all these muted days,
If it meant I was with you.

I Remember —(A Victim's Lament)

I remember
      your knife glinted in the dying light
      as I took my last breath
      on
      that trembling winter day.
      when the frost sparkled in the dim
      of the early morning.

I remember
      the sound of the birds
      echoing my screams
      as they sung each other lullabies
      to banish the night from their sleepy eyes,
      their hush awakening
            the new blooming roses
                  cascading in the wind.

I remember
      life.

Legend

In a blaze of lightning and thunder
she appears surrounded by a
cloud of well-placed fury

A leader of the death march,
ghosts having long since ascended to the halls
of myth and fairy tale.

A storm fuelled by the wings of a phoenix
Catalyst of survival,
she soars
across a rain-damp sky
starry night twinkling
in a distant galaxy
we're never destined to reach

A figment of the imagination
We can hardly remember
Staining our memory like a bruise
Too sore to touch.

Hurricane

You were born amid a tornado,
Rattling hinges and
a gust too loud for us to even hear our thoughts,
barricades sheltering families against the dark.

When the night was at its worst
You
Taught us how to find the light,
Fostered the smouldering embers within.

As the air grew cold,
Your spirit kept us warm,
With the delicate grace of a thousand suns
Beyond the cinders and the smoke

You became the wind that
Carries us on
We breathed in your oxygen and let it fill our souls
while you transformed into the Southern star
Guiding us on our way.

When twilight ushered in the night
With a blaze of pink and emerald blue
You handed me the torch

Jackie Smith

And I lit the flame of courage in a globe
Too blind to see the miracle
Of a rainbow after the storm.

As we sit back
To witness the land aglow with lies long accepted as true
I know that I am the hurricane
That will spark the change in this life,
And now,
Now is the time
To fight,
To grow,
To grow,
And drag the world along
With us
Into this new beginning.

Mystic

Stars glisten in the night sky,
slick with summer rain
shimmering with the reflection
of lakes below.

Storm clouds above whisper
haunted ghost tales
real enough to make
grown men cry
and tremble in their wake.

Lightning bugs dance –
oh, can you see them –
thickly among constellations,
welcoming werewolves
long after the full moon has gone to bed.

Witches brew poisonous tea
Plotting the death of
Would-be princesses destined for early ends
as dwarfs mine for treasure
tainted by a cursed warlock's touch.

Sleep, my dear one.
It's just a nightmare …
It's just a nightmare.
Shh …

Black Dahlia

Black dahlia,
how do you grow, when all
the world is covered in snow?

Your fallen petals turn to gold,
Smudges of ink on a blank page.

You leave your mark on this land
By following the ghosts of fractured angels,
Haloes slipped and choking.

Embrace the silence
that is still too loud,
but quieter than a whisper,

Long enough to hear your heart beat
Cease
in the final moments
when you take your last breath,
and the clocks turn backwards at noon.

Ashes

The day they took you away,
the sun lost its shine,
Autumn burned into winter
Chill air breathing smoke upon
The mountain top,
In the distance.

They stripped
Your innocence along
With the clothes you left
Discarded on the floor,
Shivering in their icy glances
And condescending sneers.

Your mottled skin shrank
against the waning light.

And I,
Too weak
To fight
Could do nothing but rage
With the fire
Of an ever-burning candle.

I let the world engulf me with its
Salty-sour waves
Crying for the injustice
Of it all,
And the hole
You left in my heart
Shattered,
Beyond repair.

New World

I don't understand
this new land
so much darker
than my own.

This world,
Your world,
Not mine
Because it will never be mine
So awkward and strange
I cannot tell
where it ends
and I begin.

I walk the streets of what is to become
my hometown
but do not see anything
that reminds me of home,
no colour on the dawn,
grey where there should be light.

Voices like thunder from a faceless
treasure chest,
Olympus Gods,

no longer drink champagne
on mountaintops
and sing the blues away.

This is Hades
a land
of fire and flame
where the sick
die young
and there is no cure
for stupidity,
no spell that can reverse time
and return to
moments fleeting.

When nymphs danced
Upon the waves and
My spirit
Ran free.

This world is not my own,
Never will be
Never could be
But it is now the
Place
I must call my home.

The End

The silence greets me like a welcome friend,
Asks me to play by the light of the moon
with an abandon not seen since childhood.

We meet,
Like the storm encounters the rainbow
Before it fades into angry sleep,
pieces falling back into place as though we
knew we belonged together all this time
magnetised, magnified by the deathly
hollow sounds outside our door,
we wait for the sinking of the
summer sun
to call time on this whirlwind innocence.

We wait.
We're still waiting …
For The End.

If You're Listening

(For Nan)

The day your heart stopped was the day
Mine became a little smaller
That phone call with the pitied sighs and
Silences that seemed to go on forever.
And I felt time as I knew it come to a
Screeching halt as my spirit slowly shattered
Into a million tiny little pieces

I became a void nothing could fill
An empty cup
An oasis dying of thirst
As every memory we created together
Washed over me
To fill the space you'd left behind
Your laugh
Your smile
Your touch

Fingertips leaving bruises on skin
A wound that never heals,
Exposed to the elements,
The sin of salt rubbed in to make every passing moment
Just that little bit harder to bear

As I walk through this day
This life
Without you.

They say your heart is a muscle,
The beating life force of your soul growing from within.
With a slow
Thrump
thrump
thrump
it throbs,
Shepherding blood through veins,
The cortex of a body not meant to last forever,
And when it stops you no longer remain
Here on Earth.

But with each year comes understanding,
An acceptance and a desire to carry on as though
You were still with me.

So I've broken down these barriers,
Let the walls come tumbling around me with a crash

I've followed the plans we
Once made together and watched
As the stars slowly unite
And all my far-off dreams have come true.

I've let your fading soul fill me with a guiding light
Even Death could not contain,
Taken the flag of surrender and turned it into a
Badge of courage fuelled only by your love.

And as I lay down at night,
To the echoing
thrump
thrump
thrump
of my
Own shadowed heart
Sometimes I feel you near,
Reach for you and find an empty bed.

If you're listening
If you're out there
Somewhere,
sharing your endless glow
With someone who needed it more than I,

Then I hope I've made you proud.

Sunrise

What I remember of that summer dawn
The days when spring turned shy
was the flowers as they danced
delicate and high
above
the rainbows,
and the bright new sun.

Pink with the promise of what was yet to come,
Blue with the sadness of what's left behind
Yellow in this memory
Where hope still shines.

These colours float around us,
And I'm forever yours
Caught in your dazzling crimson glow
Vibrant as a rose.

While I am violent blue,
Deep purple in the grey,
Lost in the black sapphire of the moon's lingering haze
Wondering how I ever deserved a love
So true,
Long
And everlasting.

Sunlight

Rose coloured glasses may block out the sun, but they do not hide the cracks in your mask. You lurk in the shadows of the early morning grey, hide in the darkness of midnight. But even in the pitch black I see you. The full moon shines like glitter on your waning light and I cannot see anything but you. Your ghostly silhouette is radiant. I just wish you could see it.

Heirloom

If there were an heirloom
I could claim as my own
it would be the ring you gave me
for my birthday one year.

I never took it off.

Two hearts intertwined with gold,
you said it was so we'd never be apart
that the sparkle of the stones
reflected your love,
and how you would always be there for me.

Now many years have passed and that summer
Has long since faded.

I can no longer call your name in times of trouble,
and expect a response,
only the echoes of your spirit that
somehow lives within the soul,
in memories of a house long abandoned
when your time came for
eternal sleep.

And still I wear this ring
I never took it off.
It's two sizes too small
But I'll never take it off,
Because it reminds me of your love
And how it's ever present,
Even though you're gone.

Grave of Yesterdays

On this grave of all our yesterdays
Leave flowers in place of regret,
Pull the weeds and tend to trees
Start to bloom again.

Keep your second chances close
To your heart
Jump from the waterfall even if you can't swim.

I'll take these broken silences
And make them whole
With tape and safety pins,
Harness the power of the uncontrollable and speak
All these thoughts within.

I'll catch these stolen moments,
Where we've created peace and stopped time
Build a future from ashes of the fire.

Stop the storm at the first spark of lightning
Before the thunder starts a war.

I'll remind myself when the world turns grey
the endless colour that lies within.

Warrior

I stand here exposed before you,
Buckled knees,
Posture imperfect
shoes unlaced
but not for lack of trying.
And I am always trying.

I wasn't made to blend in.
Underneath these clothes, my
skin is a canvas of old bruises,
mottled yellow green with age.

I trace my finger along every broken scar,
Chipped tooth a memory of childhood
Where I ran so fast
Because I believed I could,
Jumped from the highest waterfall of prismatic beauty,
Just because you knew I would,
Not take no for an answer
When I asked you if I could fly.

Fly high,
I'm soaring now,
Above the treetops
And into the grey light of the fading moon
As it shares its secrets with the noon-day sun,
Hidden in the shadows
Of a desolate blue,
Cloudy sky.

See, where you look at me,
And shy away,
Cringe at marks on skin,
An awkward gait
That is not like yours,
I see promise,
Endurance,
A willingness to
Never give up,
Even though you told me I can't.

Each bruise left on skin by tainted words
And good intentions
Has made me who I am today
A warrior in a world
Caught up in what cannot be achieved
Instead of the possibility
Of what can.

So I stand before you,
Naked,
Battle scarred
And bruised,
To let you know that
I will not give up,
Can't, won't and never will.

Don't count me out just yet.

Warrior Pt 2

I am more than the
patchwork quilt of scars
that cover tender skin,
the sharp shape of me
that refuses to
bend to your will.

You may have left your mark
on me,
through acid laced words
designed to injure
but I told you not to
count me out just yet.

3 2 1
… and I'm still standing.

Words have become my armour,
an army to follow me.
I built it piece by piece
Until I was strong enough
to deflect every barb you throw at me,
counter every bullet with one of my own.

And now, like a moth to the flame
I always find my way home
long after the candle is extinguished.

A night sky overcast with clouds
may look like an inky canvas
but remember that even the sleepiest stars still shine,
will burn at the touch
if you get too close.

I told you I'm a warrior now,
Strike me if you dare.

Free Falling

In this delicate moment before it begins,
there is silence too loud
to hear a pin drop as
I ride the crushing waves of
Chaos.

I leaped without a parachute
Screamed in a whisper
and still expected they would
catch me
as I fell
from grace
from safety
from belief
in every single thing
I thought I knew
To be true.

Like you didn't just
Trample my heart
With your well-meaning words
Shatter my existence with your tongue,
Tones soothing yet so
Much more than condescending.

My skin feels too tight,
For this body
So awkward and frail.

But they don't notice
Simply watch as I burn
From within
Pale complexion
Dyed crimson
With your sweet, stinging
Turn of phrase.

I am drowning
In the echo of the ocean,
And they remain on shore
Waving, frolicking against
The summer skyline.

Count their blessings
One by one
that their mothers taught
Them how to swim
With the tide
Rather than against.

And then,
The heart slows
And this delicate,
Ungraceful,
Messy,
Beautiful moment
In which I took a chance
For once
On the unknown
Becomes one
With the fabric
Of the past
So we all
Move on.

White on White

1.
It all began with a mattress
Returned in flashbacks sparking a fever dream
Humming in the pale moonlight
Crumpled skin in the early hush of the morning
Half asleep but vibrating with the promise of
Waking
Unfurling like a flower
To welcome the sun.
White on white.

2.
No sound
But our breath
Tangled in the silence
I traced every inch of your delectable skin
With my tongue,
Watched the hairs on your arms stand to my attention
Echoed the shadows you cast across silk
In the rise and fall of friction that fuelled our fire.

3.

We kissed
And I
Not knowing that it would be our last
Failed to savour the taste of you on my cherry lips
Salt rimmed and frosted glass
Sugared honey doused in cinnamon
Like a rose
In bloom.

4.

We were a candle always
Meant to burn out but
You opened me up
To a world
I never knew
Taught me how to paint in shades of
the palette I thought impossible
Guided my hands to the fragile
Pink of the clouds in the fractured blue sky above

5.

Soft and round at the curve
Together we found their shape
Sharp like lightning after the thunder.
Forever wanting
Forever waiting
For the rain to fall.

6.

Masked in the darkness as stars wake from dreams
You found me lost
And alone in a forest blacker than the Devil's soul
You brought me into the light
Now all that's left of your Prescence
Is a faded sweat-stained outline of your perfect
Indigo body
On this old mattress
And the glow of your haloed ghost
In the evening.
White on white.

Code Breaker

We speak in code names
only decipherable between us,
gesture like mimes who have lost
their ability to sign.

We treat the world like it's a puzzle,
A word jumble,
Written in a language we don't understand,
a sudoku when we can't count numbers after 6,
a jigsaw missing a piece that never really fit.

Sacred heart, you saw me
In the darkness,
Followed the ghosts of my past

Didn't shy away from my rising voice,
Didn't guide my hand when I failed to colour between the lines.

You see the mystery within, and explore its depths
With me

You trace the glitter in my scars as you listen to the rattle
Of silence on my tongue.

You know me,
And for that I love you.

Black Flamingo

Black flamingo,
why do you cry,
is it because wherever you go,
shadows follow in your wake.

I see their barbs cut deeper
than a knife,
you hide your wounds well,
behind onyx feathers
and moonstone-coloured eyes.

But I see you,
Beyond your dark wings,
your heart made of gold,
warmer than the sun
rich as a king,
just itching for a chance
to be loved.

So take my hand, dear one,
and we'll show them how it's done,
soar higher than anyone ever has,
touch the stars
and lose ourselves in the waters
of the milky way.

Remember beauty like yours
is as rare as the desert rose on
an ocean wave.

You shimmer with all the light
the world has to offer,
speak to the darkness the way
no one else can.

Amid stormy weather
Knocking at a ship's cabin,
You are the compass guiding us
to a safe haven.

When all seems lost,
and you cannot find your way,
remember you are the light
that guides us home.

Remember you are our home.

I Wish I Were A Feather

I wish I were a feather,
flying high upon the breeze,
I'd soar through treetops,
visit lands unexplored,
bathe in the waters of untapped lakes
and swim under glistening waterfalls.

I'd dance along the stars,
counting them one by one
hold tight to the comet's tale,
and when the day is done,
I'd fall back to Earth
to be by your side,
forever more.

I wish I were a feather.

Daffodils

We paint the walls the colour of daffodils,
(Your favourite shade of hope),

We close the door of your room never used,
Keep the light where it belongs.

Shattered hearts concealed by unblemished skin,
Ignore the decay within.

Make up covers the tears we cry,
At night when memories overwhelm.

In this house we now live as ghosts,
Passing ships in the night.

In the morning, birds no longer sing for us,
Can't find joy in the melancholy.

This pain is all encompassing now,
It bites and itches at our façade.

For what are we without you now,
Who fills the hole you should have been in?

Echoes in the Vibration

Your sadness echoes in the vibration
Of rain against the windowpane
Tears falling
As you cry to the new moon,
Pray to a forever sun
I know this hurt kills you,
Slowly bleeding the lifeforce of your soul.
And I wish there was something I could do,
But there's not,
Never was,
Never will be
So I take your hand,
Whisper quiet words to soothe you as the storm clouds gather overhead
And one day, maybe soon
That will be enough.

Wait for Me

Wait for me,
oh fair princess,
on the corner of
yesterday and tomorrow.

Where clocks pause
And time stops,
So I can meet you
      Again and again,
           Over and over.
Like it was the first time,
For the rest of our lives.

Your rags may be in tatters
But I only need your smile.

I will mend this shattered heart
of yours
with needle and thread
careful as can be, I'll make my stitch,

Until the clock strikes midnight,
And it's déjà vu all over again.

Martyr (Joan of Arc)

With the windows open,
fire on high,
I am blind,
trapped in this padded cell
of my own making.
Static clouds masking my thoughts,

an ever-interrupting frequency of a song
I will never hear the ending to.
A story unfinished,

a symphony unwritten
and here I lie,
shattered and empty,
with the windows open,
fire on high.

On the floor,
in pieces like glass
too fragile for your touch,
fragments of a reality you
refuse to accept …

would rather live in the fantasy of your own creation.

And still I remain here,
Choking,
With the windows open,
fire on high
Burning to ash.

Watch me soar,
Like a phoenix.

I am the boxer
in the shadows,
the darkness calls my name.

They will remember me,
in the eclipse,
when they're lost by the harvest moon,
and it seems that there's no one
left to fight.

I stand
For injustice,
For the minority.

They will turn to me
For I am the broken porcelain you left on the pavement,
Trod on and covered with dirt.

I am the mirror you can't look into,
For fear of acknowledging your own evil.
And you can douse all our candles,
Burn me at the stake,
Still I will shimmer,
Forever lighting the way.

I Am

I am not your marionette,
dancing on a string.

I am not your delicate flower
to be sheltered from the rain

I am not your puzzle,
Only one answer will solve.

I am not your inspiration,
No karma to be claimed.

I am more than this world has to offer,
Sharp edges in a round globe.

I was not made to fit in your box,
They taught me to look beyond.

I am the wanderer,
Spark to the flame.

I am the voice of the voiceless,
Listen and you will hear.

I am human,
Just like you.
If you cut me I will bleed.

Glitter

I measure my love
by the light,
the light that shines from your eyes
like diamonds made from
the coal dark night
as starbursts shower our dreams
with their glimmering promise.

Forever

We swim in oceans,
Brimming with love
dance in the spotlight
of a glowing sun.

A glowing sun,
We follow the rainstorm
Discover pots of gold
in the desert
in the city
in all the clouds above.

In all the clouds above,
We take our greatest joy,
Sing with the angels
Perfect harmonies in the score.

With perfect harmonies in the score,
we take heart in love and lace,
delicate in its fragility
for every step forward with you is a step towards forever.

… forever.

Call Me

If, in the starry night,
Black til morning dawns,
you seek balance in a world off kilter with the universe,
Call me,
A dozen times,
Reach out to me,
As the stars fold upon each other
      And explode into the startling chaos we can only
                      Describe as
A miracle.

Take my hand,
As the dust settles upon the ancient spring
Where oases are few and far between
Call me,
In the distance,
When you no longer know what to do.
And I will show you the light;
Guide you on your way.

On Existence

We haunt the houses of strangers
travel through forgotten hallways
and rooms time has left untouched.

We speak to no one
              at least not the living –
leave our thumbprints on other people's history.

We walk the darkness over hallowed ground
as even the sleepiest star in the midnight sky
shines overhead,
and hope that we will be remembered,
if not by those who love us,
then just by someone
    anyone
in proof that we lived.
We existed.
And it wasn't all for nothing.

Mute

Bleed in purple, blue and grey
as inky fingerprints trace a map on untouched skin,
permanent, like a trail of bruises over the heart,
darker than sin.

Wounds weep in yellow, indigo and green,
an ever-changing pattern,
you left your mark on me.

And now I look in the mirror,
hidden from the light,
eyes shadowed black with the tears I cried.

If no one can hear me,
did I even really scream?

Songbird

Little songbird,
Your song is so melancholy
I hear your cries on the wind,
A forgotten melody
Nobody knows how to sing.

Sing, sing, little songbird,
This is your time.
Fly high,
Shimmer as the sun folds into the everlasting distance.

Wildfire

It's dark
Blacker than the inky charcoal
that has been left behind after the flame has burnt out.

In these moments of silence
I am suspended
In the grips of time before the music starts with
A slow heavy percussion echoing
The slow heavy beat of my heart
Measuring the seconds between each breath
That recognise when possibilities are endless and Dreams,
All these weary dreams
Have a chance to become
The reality they were born to be.

The Enigma

Kohl dark eyes
And a serpent's tongue,
She exudes the strength of an army
The force of a hurricane,
Leaving destruction and mangled bodies
In her wake
The poor pray to her alter,
The smart know when to look away,
Curse the sound of her name
As the Enigma comes out to play,
Suck the lifeforce out of woman and child,
Bleeding veins until they're dry
And as the night blends into the morning,
She fades into the shadowy night.

This Place

This place is awash with memory
this grass the place I learned to fall
without grace
and watched the stars inherit the sky
as it sparkles with diamonds.

This place is where the sun
Became the moon,
dawn became dusk

This is the place where I
Learned to run
instead of walk
towards a future
I cannot imagine.

This is the place where the flowers
turned to grey,
This is the place where I learned to love
at midnight,
in the middle of the day,
when the light has turned to rain
we taste on tongues.

This is the place that reminds me
Of you
and will forever be
My home.

Mathematics of Courage

If life is an equation
y equals you and all the possibilities of tomorrow
that only exists in your presence
I am x with dreams to take on challenges much higher than my reach.

Let crimson summers in the dawn of the winter as the sun
peeks through the shadowed curtains
spark memories of yesterday
and all that you told me could be achieved if
I was only brave enough to try.

Those highborn mountains
touch the sky shrouded in the mist
of the god's magic
because they saw no barrier between
Earth and whatever exists beyond the heavens.

We dance at twilight under twinkling stars because night
does not always herald the end of the day if I'm not finished
drinking in these fragile moments
we capture in sonnets.

As the solar eclipse plunges the world into darkness
I remember that silhouettes remain
sparkling and new
shining with all the light that burns so bright
even the blind
can harness its power.

If life is an equation,
you represent y and I x
I won't linger in the knowledge that you are no longer
here to see all my wishes come true,
because your courage showed me
what could be
if I only dared to dream.

Selway Avenue

When I think of your home
I think not of the space you occupied before you
Left the world for an early grave,
Not the room that held the aura of you,
Too many clothes in the closet
And shoes you haven't been able to wear for years.

Home was the place we visited on holidays,
Yellow brick and stairs made of tile,
Chipped at the edges from age,
Hurried feet wearing colour from carpet.

The kitchen where we all gathered at Christmas,
Heavy with happiness and light as we all returned
To the castle we called our kingdom.

The chair in the corner where Grandfather used to sit,
I don't remember the imprint of his smile,
As your cheeks turn red,
Only know it was true from worn out images stained with our
    fingerprints
As we knitted together the moments that made up our past.

The living room where I took first steps unaided age 9
Where you watched on beaming with pride,
Knowing that nothing
Nothing could ever
Stop me from making dreams come true

Home is not home without you in it,
Home is the warmth of your sacred arms around my waist,
Pulling me in tight so my body could mould itself to yours.

It's the sound of your laugh
When I told a joke
No one else found funny,
Dances choreographed in the front yard
to the latest pop release
we declared was the
Best Song Ever.

Home
Was the touch of your hand,
The pulse of your spirit
I keep within my heart
Forever and forever on.

I'll keep your soul close and ensure
It's spark,
Forever and ever
Lives on.

Lost in a Lullaby

(After Lewis Carroll's Alice in Wonderland)

In the darkness of the midnight hour,
Before the sky becomes light with the hazy blush of
The sun
As it fades like the last rose in Autumn,
I witness the moon become nothing more
Than a sliver,
In the deep, endless void of night,
Like the Cheshire cat's smile
As he teased Alice with the wonder of puzzles and riddles
She was never really meant to solve
.
Sometimes I feel like Alice,
Duty bound with valour
to protect a heart I never knew was breaking
The wind filled with a sorrow it cannot name,
Heavy with the promises we've left unfulfilled,
Trampling houses made of cards as we seek shelter under trees
Made desolate with the early arrival of Winter.

The Dead Sea comes alive with bodies better left
Below.
They leech blood from veins,

The way ravenous butterflies seek out
The sticky nourishment of the sweetest flower in June.
Pulsing heartbeat on pause.

When the planets hide behind a cloud
And all that's left is the repressive hunger of a heat
That lingers
Like an eternal flame.

But in the morning
I will wake,
Bleary eyed and reckless smile
From the Caterpillar's burnt-out cigarette
Safe in a bed I call my own
And the knowledge
That this,
Endless rampant spiral we
Call a nightmare
Was nothing more than a daydream.

Wasn't it?

Nightmare

This is the sound of my nightmares,
filling the corners of darkness each night as I try to sleep.

A deep desolate hum
    Moving   ever   closer
    With each second
That passes until it is
            So close
I can barely breathe;
its force
like a rough wave
too deep to tread water.

So I succumb to the rising panic,
Have faith in the promise that is
just a bad dream
and tomorrow …
I shall see the sun once more.

Speed of Sound

This heart of mine
Beats
To the speed of sound
The ratio of light
    Bouncing
        Bouncing
From one corner
    Of my imagination
To the next
Never ending.

Too Late

Dear future flower children
Who took God's promise that they shall inherit the earth at face value.
While you danced under a halo of solar glory,
We set the world alight and watched it burn
Allowed the grass beneath your bare feet turn grey with neglect,
As the sky rained upon us from above.

I'm sorry we did not speak when
we thought no one would listen
left the talking to those whose intentions
weren't as good as once promised,
ignored the ticking clock,
not recognising that in my hands I held
a bomb.

Broken Wing

I get lost in the horizon
Of the winter dawn
Cascading colours
In the shade of the rainbow
Party beyond this morning light
Pale against the snow
Lighter than the feather
That falls from wings
not meant for flying.

Storybook Affair

If a look is the spark of love to last a lifetime,
        and beyond,
every glance you send my way turns me to kindling,
and together,
we breathe in the flame
of a glorious romance surpassing fairy tales
and legends of childhood,
where you are the knight
slaying the dragon,
        and I am the lonely princess trapped
in a tower.
We'll save each other
    In the end.

Paradox

I cry volumes
At the waves as they crash
Upon the midnight shore
Violent yet calming
A paradox like no other
As I contemplate all that has
Led me here
To this dying road
Where the beginning
Meets the end,
And there is no in-between.

Worthy

I measure my worth
By the light,
The light that shines
From his eyes like diamonds
Made from the coal dark night
While starbursts
Shower our dreams with their promise
Of an existence much greater
Than our own,
The assurance that life
Is for the living
And a minute wasted is sixty
Seconds of air
That you cannot breathe
Again.

We waltz under trees ignited by the moonlight
Indulge
In a universe
Of us that has
No meaning
Beyond the beating of our hearts,
Fingerprints on skin,
To skin as we trace

Our lifeblood
Back to the start,
Again and again
Within
And without,
Forever.

Flickering Flame

These voices shriek and moan
Mimic the sturdy vibration of
My thrumming fingertips upon
Solid surface
while I swim through the bouts of an
ocean so deep and dark
breaking the surface feels impossible.

I'm swept away by the turmoil of restless fantasies
A silence I can't explain
As I spiral
      Down
            Down
                  Down.

But when I wake,
Light is crystal blue
Clearing shadows from eyes
The sky is the colour of a bruise
But I don't linger
In my inevitable demise

For at night when all is inky black
And I can't see the sun
For the flickering flame
A new day comes with clarity
A miracle
Of what remains
And from these ashes I will stand

Burnt tinder doused in smoke
To fight the demons of my dreams
And keep my enemy from the door.

Impossible

Nothing is impossible. The word itself says "I'm possible."
— Audrey Hepburn

They shriek the word impossible,
like it's a threat and not a challenge

Like impossible hasn't been met on stony steps
in protest to what cannot be
shouted from rooftops as the sky turns dark,
becoming shields against a dying force
you cannot believe.

Impossible that we can fly to the moon,
Journey across oceans
Sleep among stars
And still not see that what was once Impossible
Is now possible
if we only believe
in impossible possibilities,

Like if you shout the word impossible on an abandoned mountain tops
Shrouded in shades of starlight grey
They will always echo back the words
"I'm possible."

Madness

If we,
(Reckless with this love)
counted all the colours in a desert storm
abandoning all hope of finding a non-existent
ocean,
how long would it be
until we reached infinity?

Do you know why light shines brightest in the depth
Of midnight,
cursing winters with a hallowed glow,
a mystery that can't be
explained away by childhood fantasies
and an overactive imagination

Do you know why
Cries
Seem loudest when there's no one to hear
You scream,
Only the self-imposed despair echoing off
Your dungeon walls
As we take hesitant steps towards a
Future no one can predict
Or guarantee.

Mother Nature

I want to take these
Silent steps
Towards tomorrow
And linger amongst the trees
As though they have something to teach me.

As though all Mother Nature
has learned can be imparted
through the blossoming
of a new flower,
when we rest a moment
to listen
for the whisper
of her voice on the rustling leaves,
while the rain falls
and washes the world clean.

There is much we could learn
From a heart filled,
With such wisdom.

Bouquet

The sky is full of flowers
Lavender hues of the setting sun
collapse into black darkness sprinkled
with baby's breath.

In the morning,
There are roses,
A blushing pink bouquet as welcome
As the chrysanthemum crystal skies.

These wildflowers I gift to you
With everything I have
And everything I am.

Tread carefully,
Mind the weeds.

Pedestal

(After Neil Hilborn)

I'm a collector of confused stares,
pitying looks and sympathetic smiles.

Hellos turn into platitudes,
simpering whispers of pride and inspiration.

I am a collector of the destitute,
languish in the poverty
of your gaze.

Empty eyes and wilful lies,
shrouded in your praise.

I never asked to be put upon this pedestal,
but from it I will rise.

You will look up at me,
and wonder at just how far I've come,
Can't you see what I have done?

Proved wrong all the cynics,
the naysayers who said I can't.

From up here in the clouds,
I see it all much clearer now.

The world is my oyster and
I'll sing much louder now
join the chorus of angels as they welcome the sun
and when the darkness comes
I'll return to Earth to remind you
I am no god.

Not someone to be admired,
Consoled or trod upon.

I am human just like you,
and from these scars I bleed.

Spirit

Sunlight splinters through charcoal smudged skies
Like the shattered hearts of many a visitor
as autumn storms wash neglected tombstones
clean,
dirt-stained emeralds in a coal-laden mine.

We chase the ghosts of ancestors passed,
Follow whispered memories along open-air hallways
sustained by ancient trees growing taller as each century turns.

This is not what I imagined when I think of death
No pearly gates,
No heavenly Nirvana becoming full circle
in the resurrection
of good deeds
spent across a lifetime …
so long
and yet …
Never long enough.

What I wouldn't give for
another minute
another second
another moment

of time if I could spend it
in quiet reflection
the loving embrace your Prescence provided.

But here,
Among the cobwebs
and leaves
I find an inner peace
Knowing
That while this is where
Your chalk-like bones may find their final resting place
Your spirit,
Your soul
And all you taught me
Resonates
In us,
In me,
In everyone who loved you.

Because we all loved you,
Dearly.
I still love you
Dearly.

Symphony

I hear your song in the bird call
Melody
unhurried resonance on the breeze,
like a piano introduction,
harmony of violins
as they unite in the chorus.

And in the rising crescendo
I see your silhouette;
It lights up the shadows,
Rainbows dance upon the ceiling
As though on tiptoe
to the hollow beat
of your drums.

But if there ever comes a day
When I listen for your voice
Only to hear
The return of silence
I'll know the time
has come
to join

the choir
in everlasting sleep,
walk over the bridge,
beyond the light.

I'll see you
in my dreams.

Perfect Imperfections

I wish
I could have seen the beginning of time,
Tuned this radio dial to somewhere that wasn't here,
Into a station light years away,
Where nothing else mattered but the untouched sun rotating around
The moon
Playing tango with the night.

I wish
I could have heard that moment when,
Out of the silence,
The static itself came alive with the spark of a billion stars
Waking from wishes not yet made as the angels painted their idea of heaven among
The clouds in all the shades of their endless imagination
Spun the halo round Saturn
Because sometimes we need a reminder that we too can shine.

I wish
I could have been there when man first walked on the moon,
And we danced feather-light and free.

I wish

I could have witnessed the blue sea turn red against the reflection
Of your waves,
When they parted water to make way for a ubiquitous god
Who only wanted to walk in the rain.

I wish
I had seen
It all,
That I believed in the strength
it takes to have faith in the unknown
Because then I would harness the power to remove
The hurt
From your eyes when they look up at me from shallow graves.

I wish I
Could find the words to tell you how beautiful I think you are,
How beautiful I am
In all my perfect imperfections
And embrace all the tiny pieces of this reckless soul
To create an armour
Against a universe that tells me I
Am not
good enough.

Because today,
I am good enough.

Aurora

Your words leave bruises on my heart
the colour of mulberry wine in Summer.
Fingerprints running over scars long healed,
Sharp, quick witted as you tear at the seams
So you can see the bullet holes you left behind.

You,
With your restless smile and acid tongue
Sought to wound where it hurt the most,
Picked at the cracks in my skin so you could find the
Weak spots.

You, with your ice-laden sentences and steel-like glares,
Knife's edge and monochrome heart.

But I,
I've stitched together the patchwork rubble
You made of me
Piece by piece, inch by inch in a flare of endless colour.

Until there's nothing,
Nothing left of us,
Nothing left of me
But the knotted fabric you neglected,
All frayed and threadbare with your lies.

You see,
I'm no longer who I used to be,
I've grown a lot since then.
Solidified those parts of me that bent to your will like
The waves of a fragile sea.
You may be ice,
But I am the fire,
The fire that follows the lightning in the storm
Filled with fury in a hurricane
Setting ablaze the wreckage you abandoned
In your haste for a better view.

I am the gilded sun
The goddess of light,
The ember you left to ignite,
The Aurora you seek to worship
At the rising of the new morning.

Come closer
Warm your weary bones by
My heady glow,
Safe in my sacred arms,
Let my lullaby welcome you into dreams.

Touch me,
and I'll watch you burn
become one with the starlight
as it stirs in the sleepless sky.
I said I'd have my revenge;
Don't say I didn't warn you.

Notes

Some of the poems featured in this collection are written in response to photographs, paintings and other poems I have read as part of writing workshops. By including their titles and authors here and within the book, I am acknowledging that inspiration.

Blind Ballerina (After Alicia Alonso) – this poem was written after I saw an image of Alicia Alonso and read a little about her history.

https://artsandculture.google.com/entity/alicia-alonso/m0886vd?hl=en

Apocalypse (After Robert Frost) – this poem was written in response to Robert Frost's *Fire and Ice*

https://www.poetryfoundation.org/poems/44263/fire-and-ice

The Fall of Icarus (After Bruegel) – this poem is an ekphrastic written in response to Bruegel's painting *Landscape with the Fall of Icarus*.

https://www.pieterbruegel.org/landscape-with-the-fall-of-icarus/

Blank Page – this poem was written in response to both Ross Gay and Gwendolyn Brooks' poems *Sorrow is not my name*. It uses the first line "sorrow is not my name".

https://www.poetryfoundation.org/poems/92472/sorrow-is-not-my-name

Lost in a Lullaby (After Lewis Carroll's Alice in Wonderland) – this poem was inspired by *Alice in Wonderland*, written by Lewis Carroll.
https://www.goodreads.com/book/show/60671823-alice-s-adventures-in-wonderland

Pedestal (After Neil Hilborn) – this poem was written in response to work by Neil Hilborn
https://neilhilborn.com/

Acknowledgement

I would also like to take this opportunity to thank my mentor and friend, Neil Hilborn, for endorsing this poetry book. It means so much to me, and I really appreciate it.